Maplewood Public Library
7550 Lohmeyer Ave
Maplewood, MO 63143

NO LONGER PROPERTY
OF MAPLEWOOD
PUBLIC LIBRARY

Earth's Changing Climate

Habitats and Climate Change

World Book
a Scott Fetzer company
Chicago

For information about other World Book publications, visit our website at www.worldbook.com or call 1-800-WORLDBK (967-5325).

For information about sales to schools and libraries, call 1-800-975-3250 (United States) or 1-800-837-5365 (Canada).

© 2016 (print and e-book) World Book, Inc. All rights reserved. This volume may not be reproduced in whole or in part in any form without prior written permission from the publisher.

WORLD BOOK and the GLOBE DEVICE are registered trademarks or trademarks of World Book, Inc.

World Book, Inc.
180 North LaSalle Street
Suite 900
Chicago, Illinois 60601
USA

Library of Congress Cataloging-in-Publication Data
Title: Habitats and climate change.
Description: Chicago: World Book, a Scott Fetzer company, [2016] | Series: Earth's changing climate | Includes index.
Identifiers: LCCN 2015028045 | ISBN 9780716627081
Subjects: LCSH: Nature--Effect of human beings on--Juvenile literature. |
  Global environmental change--Juvenile literature. | Climatic changes--Juvenile literature. | Biogeography--Climatic factors--Juvenile literature.
Classification: LCC GF75 .C454 2015 | DDC 577.27--dc23
LC record available at http://lccn.loc.gov/2015028045

Earth's Changing Climate
ISBN: 978-0-7166-2705-0 (set, hc.)

Also available as:
ISBN: 978-0-7166-2718-0 (e-book, ePUB3)

Printed in China by Toppan Leefung Printing Ltd., Guangdong Province
2nd printing August 2016

Staff

Writer: Edward Ricciuti

Executive Committee

President
Jim O'Rourke

Vice President and
Editor in Chief
Paul A. Kobasa

Vice President, Finance
Donald D. Keller

Vice President, Marketing
Jean Lin

Director, Human Resources
Bev Ecker

Editorial

Director of Digital Product
Content Development
Emily Kline

Manager, Science
Jeff De La Rosa

Editors, Science
Will Adams
Echo Gonzalez

Administrative Assistant
Annuals/Series Nonfiction
Ethel Matthews

Manager, Contracts &
Compliance (Rights &
Permissions)
Loranne K. Shields

Manager, Indexing Services
David Pofelski

Digital

Director of Digital Product
Development
Erika Meller

Digital Product Manager
Lyndsie Manusos

Digital Product Coordinator
Matthew Werner

**Manufacturing/
Production**

Manufacturing Manager
Sandra Johnson

Production/Technology
Manager
Anne Fritzinger

Proofreader
Nathalie Strassheim

Graphics and Design

Senior Art Director
Tom Evans

Senior Designers
Matt Carrington
Isaiah Sheppard
Don Di Sante

Senior Cartographer
John M. Rejba

Acknowledgments

Alamy Images: 13 (blickwinkel), 15 (Norbert Probst, imageBROKER), 45 (Andy Holzman, ZUMA Press). Getty Images: 9 (Martin Harvey), 19 (John & Barbara Gerlach). iStockphoto: 43 (Parker Deen). Science Source: 17 (D. P. Wilson, FLPA). Shutterstock: 5 (melissaf84), 7 (Adwo), 11 (Anna Gibiskys), 25 (tamapapat), 29 (Pi-Lens), 31 (JaySi), 33 (Mogens Trolle), 35 (Courtney A Denning), 37 (Gregory A. Pozhvanov). SuperStock: 39 (Dhritiman Mukherjee, age fotostock). U.S. Fish & Wildlife Service: 23 (Olin Feuerbacher). U.S. Geological Survey: 21 (Ducks Unlimited), 41. World Wildlife Images: 27 (Greg and Yvonne Dean).

Table of contents

Introduction 4
I. Deserts
    Climate change and deserts 6
    The Namib Desert 8
    Will deserts get bigger as Earth gets hotter? 10
II. Oceans
    Climate change and ocean habitats 12
    The Great Barrier Reef 14
    Does it matter if a tiny plant or animal goes extinct? ... 16
III. Freshwater Habitats
    Climate change and freshwater habitats 18
    The Prairie Pothole region 20
    Which animals depend on freshwater habitats? 22
IV. Forests
    Climate change and forests 24
    The Amazon rain forest 26
    How do forests adjust to climate change? 28
V. Grasslands
    Climate change and grasslands 30
    The Serengeti 32
    Why are grasslands so important? 34
VI. Tundra
    Tundra and climate change 36
    Himalayan alpine tundra 38
    The warming tundra 40
VII. The Future
    Why are habitats important to humans? 42
    How can we help? 44
Glossary and resources 46
Index 48

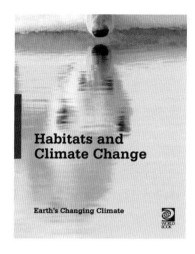

A polar bear and its reflection in the water. The ice it stands on forms a piece of the bear's habitat in the Arctic.

© blickwinkel/Alamy Images

Glossary There is a glossary of terms on page 46. Terms defined in the glossary are in type **that looks like this** on their first appearance on any spread (two facing pages).

Introduction

A *habitat* is a place that is the natural home of a living thing. It supplies food, water, and shelter for the living thing. It also provides the conditions an animal needs to *reproduce* (make more animals like itself). A habitat can be big as a desert or small as a speck of soil.

Earth and its habitats constantly change. Changes in temperature, rainfall, wind patterns, and levels of **carbon dioxide** (CO_2) in the **atmosphere** are among the forces that shape habitats. High temperatures can harm the tundra, a treeless, frozen land of the *Arctic* (Earth's farthest north region). Carbon dioxide *absorbed* (taken in) by the ocean reacts with seawater, making it more **acidic**. In acidic water, **coral reefs** can die.

Increasing levels of CO_2 in the atmosphere are leading to rising global temperatures. These temperatures cause climate change, which affects habitats around the world. Many scientists think much of the climate change is the result of human activities. Scientists worry that many plants and animals won't get used to the changes to their habitat quickly enough to be able to survive. This book discusses the problems that affect habitats as Earth's **climate** changes.

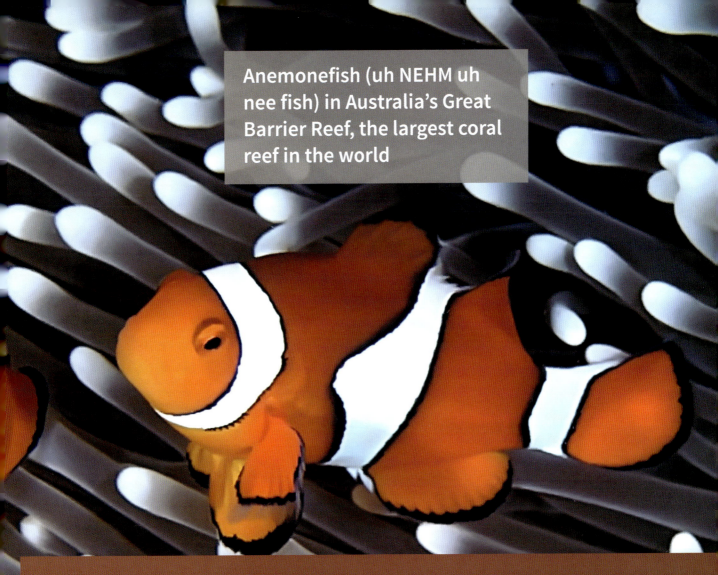

Anemonefish (uh NEHM uh nee fish) in Australia's Great Barrier Reef, the largest coral reef in the world

Global warming vs. climate change

The words *global warming* and *climate change* are often used to mean the same thing. These words are used to mean two very closely linked ideas. Global warming is the recent, *observed* (noticed) increase in **average global surface temperatures** on Earth. Climate change means the changes in climate linked to changes in average global temperature. Global average temperature has a complicated effect on climate. Global warming will not cause every place to get warmer. Instead, it will have a variety of effects on temperature, rain and snow, and other parts of climate. These effects are together called *climate change*.

I. DESERTS

Climate change and deserts

The desert is a dry habitat with few plants and animals. Desert **ecosystems** are easily harmed. Climate change can easily upset the balance of plants and animals and the habitat on which they depend. Higher temperatures, for example, may spark more frequent wildfires that destroy desert plants, which grow so slowly they may never recover their place in the ecosystem.

A desert is dry because it does not receive enough rainfall to replace the water that *evaporates* (changes to vapor and is lost). Scientists at the United Nations Environment Program predict that rainfall in many desert areas will decrease even more over the next 100 years. The predicted decrease probably results from climate change due to human activities.

Desert plants are producing more leaves. This shows that the amount of **carbon dioxide** (CO_2) in the air is increasing. Plants use CO_2 together with sunlight to make food and grow. However, the conditions favoring increased leaf growth could cause other problems. **Invasive** trees and shrubs that steal water used by desert plants and animals could thrive in areas where they once could not.

The Valley of the Moon in the Atacama Desert. This South American desert in Chile and Peru is one of the driest places on Earth.

The Namib Desert

The Namib Desert is a bone-dry strip of land, about 100 miles (160 kilometers) across at its widest. It stretches 1,300 miles (2,080 kilometers) along the Atlantic Ocean in southwestern Africa. The Namib receives less than ¾ inch (2 centimeters) of rain a year.

The quiver tree is an important **species,** or kind, of tree in the Namib desert habitat. Many insects, birds, and other small animals feed on the nectar from its large flowers. In the past, people used its tubelike branches to make holders for their hunting arrows (that is what a *quiver* is, an arrow holder). Like a cactus, the quiver tree grows slowly and lives a long time. It is well suited to the desert.

However, the change to Earth's **climate** is causing the Namib desert to become drier and hotter. As the warming increases, quiver trees in the northern Namib are dying. The quiver tree may avoid becoming **extinct** if it spreads to the southern border of its desert *range* (the geographic area in which an animal or plant species may be found). But, the quiver tree grows and *reproduces* (makes more of its kind) too slowly to do so. Experts worry that this special plant, and the many living things that depend on it, may lose its race for survival.

Fog in the Namib

The Namib is the oldest desert in the world and one of the driest. It receives little rainfall, but some areas have thick fog up to 180 days a year. The few plants and animals that make their home in this difficult habitat depend on the precious moisture in this fog, which rolls inland from sea.

Will deserts get bigger as Earth gets hotter?

Habitats that border deserts, such as grasslands, are threatened by a process called *desertification* (DEHZ uhr tuh fuh KAY shuhn). Desertification is the spread of desert habitats into surrounding habitats. Human activities, such as farming, grazing livestock, and cutting down trees, contribute to desertification. More and more, climate change plays a role as well.

Higher temperatures from global warming have dried out soils. Patterns of rainfall have changed, leaving some regions much drier. If this trend continues, the world's deserts will get larger. The Sahara in Africa, the largest desert in the world, could expand well beyond its present borders. The Sahara covers 3.5 million square miles (9 million square kilometers) across the whole of northern Africa. In places, it is already spreading 30 miles (48 kilometers) a year, replacing valuable grasslands. The Gobi, a large desert in Asia, is also spreading south into farmlands in China. The Gobi's rate of advance has been measured at up to 15.5 miles (25 kilometers) a year.

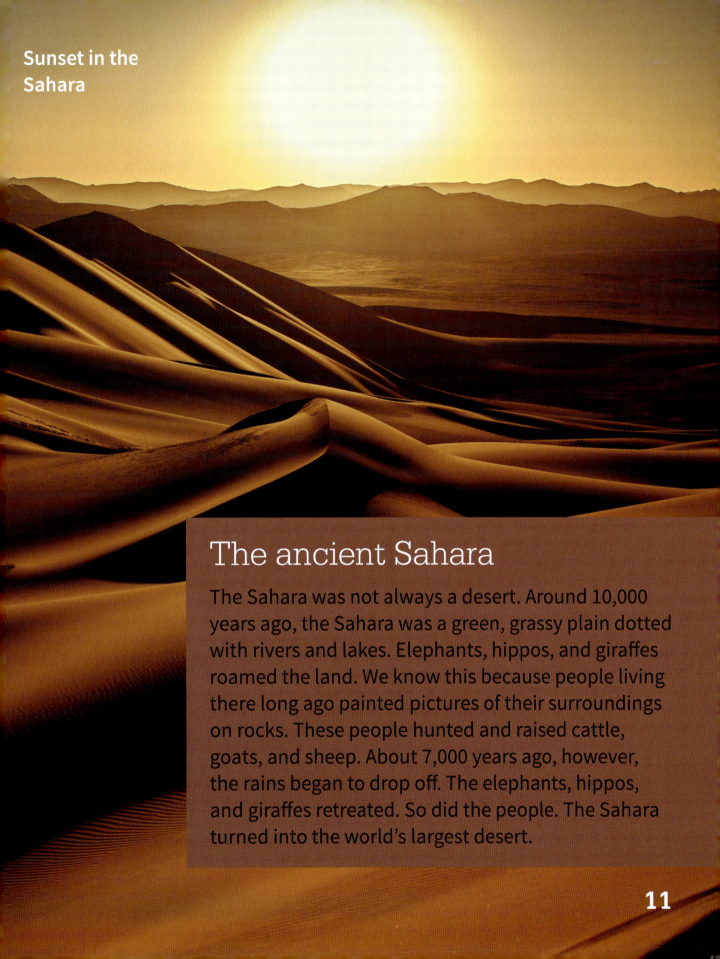

Sunset in the Sahara

The ancient Sahara

The Sahara was not always a desert. Around 10,000 years ago, the Sahara was a green, grassy plain dotted with rivers and lakes. Elephants, hippos, and giraffes roamed the land. We know this because people living there long ago painted pictures of their surroundings on rocks. These people hunted and raised cattle, goats, and sheep. About 7,000 years ago, however, the rains began to drop off. The elephants, hippos, and giraffes retreated. So did the people. The Sahara turned into the world's largest desert.

II. OCEANS

Climate change and ocean habitats

The oceans *absorb* (or take in, as a sponge does) a gas called **carbon dioxide** (CO_2) from the **atmosphere.** Animals breathe out the gas when their bodies change food into energy and living tissue. Carbon dioxide is also created by the burning of anything that has carbon. Such things include coal, gasoline, and wood.

Levels of carbon dioxide in the atmosphere doubled 56 million years ago because of huge volcanoes *erupting* (throwing out lava, ash, and CO_2). As the CO_2 reacted with seawater, oceans became more **acidic.** Living things that use calcium from seawater to make shells are especially affected by high acidity. Hardest hit were tiny one-celled animals eaten by fish. Many fish and other *marine* (ocean dwelling) animals became **extinct** because their food supply disappeared.

Today, the ocean is becoming more acid about 10 times faster than back then. Since the 1800's, people have released huge amounts of CO_2 into the atmosphere. That CO_2 is absorbed by the oceans. Many scientists worry that marine habitats will be badly harmed by this increased acidity.

A scientist studies fish on the sea floor.

The Great Barrier Reef

The Great Barrier Reef is off the coast of the state of Queensland in northeastern Australia. The reef spans about 1,900 miles (3,000 kilometers). It is not one **coral reef.** It is a string of almost 3,000 smaller ones. The enormous structure is made up of some 400 different **species** of coral.

The Great Barrier Reef is home to some 1,500 species of fish, dolphins, whales, and sea turtles. Many seabirds nest on the reef's 900 islands. But today, a one-two punch from climate change is threatening the Great Barrier Reef.

Higher water temperatures from global warming cause coral to force out the **algae** that lives in and feeds the coral. This is called *bleaching* because the coral turns white without its algae. Bleaching can kill corals. If a warm spell is temporary, corals may survive bleaching. In 1998, the highest sea temperatures ever recorded happened in the waters around the Great Barrier Reef. About half of the reef suffered bleaching.

In addition to making the planet warmer, rising levels of CO_2 are also making the ocean more **acidic.** This harms coral in building reefs. Experts worry that the Great Barrier Reef may not survive the effects of higher temperatures and ocean acidity.

Corals at the Great Barrier Reef, off the coast of Australia

Protecting the reef

The Great Barrier Reef Marine Park was established by the nation of Australia in 1975. Much of the park is off limits to fishing. No-fishing zones actually benefit fishing in the oceans. Fish that reproduce under protection help restock nearby fishing areas. Australia is planning another huge ocean *reserve* (protected area) east of the Great Barrier Reef. It will be bigger than the countries of France and Germany combined.

Does it matter if a tiny plant or animal goes extinct?

If one plant or animal goes **extinct,** it can affect many others. This is particularly true of **keystone species,** which play an especially important role in an **ecosystem.** Loss of a single keystone species can lead to the loss of many other living things in a particular habitat.

Plankton are keystone *organisms* (living things) in ocean habitats. Plankton are the many kinds of tiny plants and animals that drift in the ocean. The tiny plants are the base of the sea's **food chain.** Tiny animals eat them. Fish and other larger animals eat both. These fish, in turn, are eaten by yet other animals.

Plant plankton need nutrients, or food, to survive. These nutrients are stirred up as cold and warm water move between the ocean's surface and lower depths. But warmer water temperatures near the surface, a result of global warming, breaks up this circulation. The colder water that has more nutrients is not coming to the surface, and the plankton suffer. When plant plankton disappear, so do the many tiny animals that eat them.

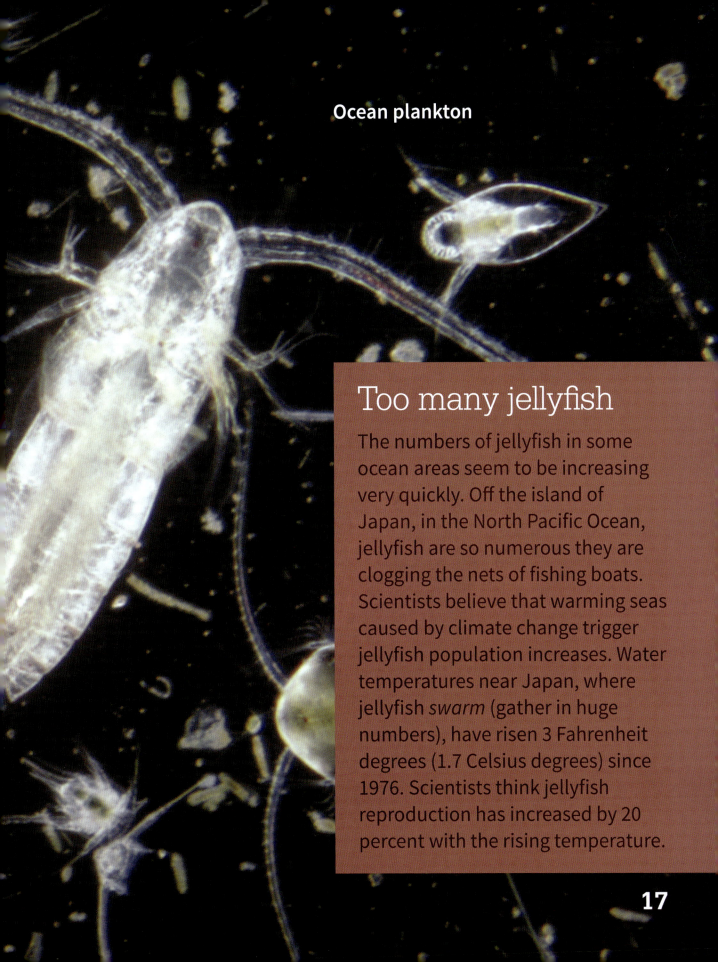

Ocean plankton

Too many jellyfish

The numbers of jellyfish in some ocean areas seem to be increasing very quickly. Off the island of Japan, in the North Pacific Ocean, jellyfish are so numerous they are clogging the nets of fishing boats. Scientists believe that warming seas caused by climate change trigger jellyfish population increases. Water temperatures near Japan, where jellyfish *swarm* (gather in huge numbers), have risen 3 Fahrenheit degrees (1.7 Celsius degrees) since 1976. Scientists think jellyfish reproduction has increased by 20 percent with the rising temperature.

III. FRESHWATER HABITATS

Climate change and freshwater habitats

Climate change can strike hard at the **ecosystems** of freshwater lakes, rivers, and **wetlands.** Often, the plants and animals that live in them are stuck with nowhere else to go. Shallow freshwater wetlands, such as swamps and marshes, are perhaps most easily harmed. They dry up quickly during **drought.**

Warming temperatures can trigger **algae** *blooms* (huge numbers of one-celled animals that grow at the same time) in lakes. Too many algae block sunlight from reaching deeper into the water. Algae that live deeper in the water do not receive enough sunlight and die. When the dead *remains* (bodies) break down, the process uses oxygen, and such fish species as trout die. Other fish that are able to live in waters low in oxygen, such as carp, take over. Such fish often eat the animals that eat algae. With fewer **predators,** algae multiply even faster.

Sometimes, frequent droughts and floods caused by climate change mean rivers may receive too much water at one time and too little at another. Wind and floodwaters carry **topsoil** into streams, especially if a drought kills the plants that hold the soil in place. Salmon are especially threated by soil clogging the streams in which they reproduce.

A Canada goose rests in a freshwater pond filled with green algae.

The Prairie Pothole region

At least 18 different kinds of water birds reproduce, feed, or take shelter for some time in the **Prairie** Pothole region of North America. Covering more than 300,000 square miles (800,000 square kilometers), the region ranges from the U.S. state of Iowa to the province of Alberta in Canada. The Pothole region is called "America's duck factory." More than half of North America's **migrating** water birds depend on this habitat for some part of their lives.

Potholes are shallow low areas in the prairie. During spring, they fill with melted snow and rain. Some hold water all year. Potholes soak up excess rainwater, preventing floods. Pothole water also seeps into the ground. Nearby farmers can tap this water for their crops.

Many scientists predict that global warming could cause longer and more severe **droughts** that will threaten the potholes. Changing weather is making western parts of the Prairie Pothole region hotter and drier. Annual rainfall has already decreased by 10 percent in some areas. The eastern region is expected to have cooler, wetter weather. However, farming has claimed most potholes there. The loss of potholes could decrease the abundance of ducks that breed there by more than half. As a result, many populations of ducks throughout North America will decrease.

Prairie Pothole region

Ice age relics

Ice age *glaciers* (massive sheets of ice) covered the pothole region until about 10,000 years ago. The potholes formed when glaciers moved north and large blocks of ice buried in the soil melted.

Which animals depend on freshwater habitats?

Threats to freshwater habitats from climate change are bad news for the millions of animals that depend on them. When people think about freshwater fish, such types as guppies, trout, or bass usually come to mind. However, many other animal groups live in freshwater habitats.

More than 1,000 types of crab are *native to* (originally from) fresh waters. Several reptiles—such as turtles, alligators, and crocodiles—live in freshwater habitats. River otters, beavers, and hippos inhabit rivers, lakes, and ponds. Songbirds, such as dippers, dive to catch small fish. Almost all **amphibians** start life in fresh water. American bullfrogs stay there throughout their lives.

Insects, such as water striders and whirligig beetles, skim on the surface of ponds and lakes. Diving beetles attack fish and tadpoles below the surface. The diving bell spider uses a bubble of air for oxygen while it hunts underwater in ponds.

Some animals live in fresh water for their entire lives. Others spend only part of their lives in fresh water. The young of the dragonfly and damselfly develop in fresh water. Adults may venture farther away, but they must return to fresh water to reproduce.

The Devils Hole pupfish is only found in one freshwater spring. That spring is in the southwestern U.S. state of Nevada.

A fragile existence

Freshwater habitats make up only 2.5 percent of the water on Earth. Even so, more than 40 percent of all fish are freshwater **species,** about 14,000 in all. Many freshwater habitats are widely separated. If the habitat of a freshwater fish species is damaged or destroyed, the fish cannot just move a little farther away. Freshwater species are very tied to the habitat in which they live.

IV. FORESTS

Climate change and forests

A forest is a habitat where trees and woody bushes are the main plants. Rainfall, temperature, and soil are among the main factors that determine what kinds of trees grow in a particular forest.

Red spruce trees need at least 36 inches (91 centimeters) of rain a year. Midsummer temperatures above 80 degrees Fahrenheit (27 degrees Celsius) are too hot for the tree. The red oak grows where rainfall is between 30 to 80 inches (76 to 200 centimeters) annually. It survives average annual temperatures from 40 degrees Fahrenheit (4 degrees Celsius) in the northern part of the range to 60 degrees Fahrenheit (16 degrees Celsius) in the southern part. Climate change will affect many forest habitats. New kinds of trees may replace those unable to survive.

Heat and **drought** increase the risk of forest fires. Many scientists think that an increase of 3.6 Fahrenheit degrees (2 Celsius degrees) in global temperature could increase the amount of forest burned by fires in the western United States by four times. Insect pests will also be a problem. Dry trees make less of the sap that helps them defend themselves against insects.

The Amazon rain forest

Rain forest habitats cover less than 3 percent of Earth. Yet they are home to more than half of all plant and animal **species.** The rain forest belt lies on both sides of the **equator.** Temperatures are always quite warm there. **Humidity** can be almost 100 percent. Some rain forests have a short dry season. But all get at least 80 inches (200 centimeters) of rain a year. Many get far more rain than that.

The Amazon rain forest, which lies across northern South America, is the largest rain forest habitat in the world. This region houses a wider variety of plant and animal life than any other place. Two and a half acres (1 hectare) of the Amazon may contain up to 280 different kinds of trees. More than 1,300 species of birds make their homes in the rain forest. The region's rivers contain up to 3,000 species of fish. Millions of insects, spiders, and other small creatures live in the rain forest. Each year, hundreds of new plants and animals are discovered there.

The Amazon forest is facing many threats from human activities. Mining, logging, and the clearing of land for farming have created treeless areas all over the rain forest. This is a problem because cutting down trees lowers the amount of water given off from leaves, decreasing rainfall and making **droughts** more severe. Climate change is expected to make occasional droughts more frequent, so rain forests could be much drier in future.

Nowhere to go

The black-breasted puffleg, a kind of hummingbird, lives only on the slopes of Ecuador's Pichincha volcano, in northwestern South America. The forest there is cloaked with clouds. The puffleg prefers cool temperatures. The bird stays higher than 9,600 feet (2,900 meters) above sea level. Today, mountain slopes are being cleared of trees for wood and farming. Climate change is also adding to the squeeze. As warmer temperatures creep upslope, the clouds go higher up the mountainside. The pufflegs must fly higher, too. But they can only go so far before they reach the peak.

Black-breasted puffleg

How do forests adjust to climate change?

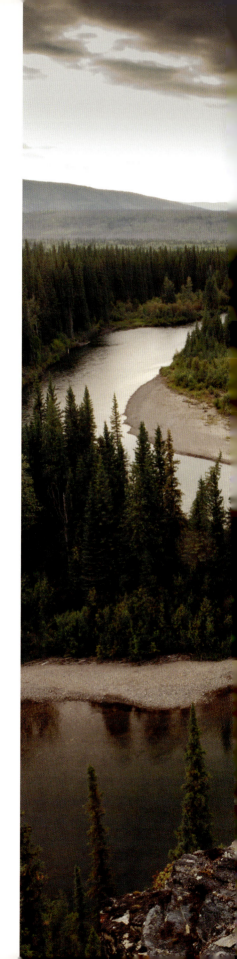

Global warming is changing the location of forest habitats on Earth. Trees are now growing on the southern edges of the *tundra* in northern Canada. Tundra is a treeless habitat where the ground is usually frozen year round. Now, **boreal** forests, made up of spruces, firs and other *conifers* (trees with needles and cones), are spreading into the thawing tundra as the **climate** grows warmer. These trees can thrive in cold—but not frozen—ground.

Although it is advancing over tundra, Canada's boreal forest is not expanding to cover more land. Its southern boundary is retreating northward. The entire forest is shifting toward the north in response to warming. Temperatures at the southern part of the forest are becoming too warm for conifers. Grasslands are taking over that land.

By the end of the century, forest near the province of Alberta, in Canada, may shift 100 miles (160 kilometers) north. But, not all kinds of trees seem able to keep up in this race against changing climate. Some species will die out.

Boreal forest wilderness in Yukon Territory, Canada

V. GRASSLANDS

Climate change and grasslands

Grasslands—open areas of grassy land with few trees—cover huge portions of Earth's surface. Grasslands grow well in areas that receive about 10 to 40 inches (25 to 100 centimeters) of rain each year. Less rain results in desert, while more rain supports forests. Most grasslands lie between deserts and more forested habitats.

Wildfires, seasonal **drought,** and grazing by large animals kill tree *saplings* (young trees), and this stops forests from invading many grasslands. Grasses turn brown in dry conditions and can even survive fire. Below ground, grass root systems escape the flames. When rains begin again, the roots spring to life with new growth.

Human activities, such as farming and raising livestock, have upset the natural balance of many grasslands. Climate change is also threatening these habitats. Global warming has increased wildfires and drought, giving grasses less time to recover. In some areas, changing wind patterns bring more rainfall, so shrubs and trees begin to replace grasses. Increased **carbon dioxide** (CO_2) in the **atmosphere,** a result of human activities, also helps these larger plants to gain a foothold in grasslands. Many grassland areas are turning into desert or forest habitats. Important native plants and animals will lost if the grassland habitat is lost.

A grassland habitat in Namibia, southern Africa

The Serengeti

One of the world's great wildlife areas is the Serengeti of northern Tanzania and southwestern Kenya. It is a vast grassland with some scattered trees. The Serengeti is home to huge populations of grass-eating animals, including antelope, buffalo, elephant, wildebeest, and zebra. It is also home to many **predators** that eat such animals, including leopards and lions.

Millions of grass-eaters gather in the southeastern Serengeti during the rainy season, December to June. The grass grows thick, and wildebeest, antelope, and zebra give birth. As the rains end, the animals begin a great **migration.** They follow the rains and green grass north. By July, they reach Kenya, where they stay until October. Then they head south again, completing the huge circle.

Climate change is now upsetting this great migration. Nowadays, heavy rains often occur over a shorter time period. As a result, flooding sometimes blocks the animals' routes. Meanwhile, the dry season is becoming longer. The wildebeest now stay longer in the north, eating all the grass faster than it can regrow. If the animals cannot move to new grass, they starve.

Zebra and wildebeest migrate across a river in Serengeti National Park, Tanzania, in eastern Africa.

Why are grasslands so important?

Fewer kinds of plants are found in grasslands than in forest habitats. The variety of animals is usually less, as well. What grasslands lack in variety, however, they make up in numbers. But many of these organisms, or living things, will struggle if grassland is replaced by desert or forest due to climate change.

Grasslands support vast populations of animals. 60 million bison, also called American buffalo, once roamed the grasslands of North America. Adult bison eat about 60 pounds (27 kilograms) of grass each day. But a healthy grassland can handle this. Bison can survive in forest habitats, but only in much smaller numbers. There is simply not enough food for them in forests.

Wide-open grasslands are ideal for birds that hunt by sight. Prairie falcons chase small birds at high speeds close to the ground. But when trees and bushes begin to grow on grasslands, it interferes with the falcon's hunting.

Many flowering plants in grasslands need lots of sun. If shaded by trees, these plants do not do well. Any animals that depend on them also suffer as a result.

A bumble bee collects pollen and nectar on a prairie flower.

VI. TUNDRA

Tundra and climate change

Tundra is a treeless habitat where much of the ground is frozen. There are two types of tundra. *Alpine tundra* forms on high mountains. At such heights, temperatures are so low that the brief warm season is too short for trees to survive. *Arctic tundra* lies in the far north. This region near the North Pole experiences long, cold winters. Summer weather rarely climbs above 50 degrees Fahrenheit (10 degrees Celsius). Trees cannot sink roots into the permanently frozen ground, called **permafrost.** Only low-lying plants and lichens, a plantlike organism made up of both **fungi** and **algae,** can grow here.

Only about 10 inches (25 centimeters) of **precipitation,** mostly snow, falls on tundra in a year. Even so, its surface is soggy. Water pools and puddles on the permafrost. Swarms of mosquitoes thrive there. Large-bodied caribou (KAR uh boo—a type of deer) dig through snow to feed on lichens and plants the year around. Smaller mammals **hibernate** during the bitterly cold winter.

But now global warming is pushing north and threatening tundra habitats. Warmer temperatures allow *non-native* (not from the area) plants and animals to move into the tundra, replacing the native *organisms* (livings things). Tundra plants and animals can move north where it is still very cold. But once they meet the Arctic Ocean, there is nowhere else to go. Alpine tundra organisms escape the warmth by moving higher, but they can only go as high as the mountain top.

Colorful Arctic tundra near the Hibiny Mountains in northern Russia

Himalayan alpine tundra

Alpine tundra is found on high mountains all over the world. It usually begins growing at about 10,000 feet (3,000 meters) above sea level, and higher on mountains closer to the **equator.** The boundary above which trees cannot grow is called the *tree line.*

In the Himalaya—mountains found in Bhutan, China, India, Nepal, and Pakistan—the tree line is around 12,000 feet (3,700 meters). Above that, such plants as mosses, bushes, and lichens hug the ground. Even higher than the alpine tundra lies the *snow line.* Above this height, no plants or animals can make a home.

Many of the animals that live on lower slopes of the Himalaya also roam the alpine tundra. Mountain sheep and the Himalayan tahr, a relative of sheep and goats, are hunted by snow leopards. Brown bears and wolves also occasionally range high into this frozen habitat.

Today, climate change appears to be reducing the amount of **precipitation** in the Himalaya. If climate change continues, the frozen alpine tundra could thaw. If rain and snow decrease and the land continues to thaw, the Himalayan tundra could become more like a desert, where few plants and animals can live.

A brief flowering

During the brief summer in the Himalaya of northern India, the Alpine tundra springs to life with blooming flowers. These plants are largely *dormant* (not active) during the long winter when snow carpets the landscape.

The warming tundra

Warming temperatures are perhaps the most worrisome part of climate change, especially in tundra habitats. Much global warming is caused by people burning **fossil fuels,** which increases the amount of **carbon dioxide** (CO_2) in the **atmosphere.** CO_2 traps heat in the atmosphere, warming Earth.

But other things also contribute to warming. One is the loss of snow cover in the Arctic. Bright snow and ice in the Arctic reflect sunlight back into space, so that sunlight does not warm the Earth. If the snow melts, the darker soil underneath absorbs more sunlight and releases it as heat, warming the air.

Also, huge amounts of CO_2 and methane (another **greenhouse gas**) frozen in Arctic tundra **permafrost** for thousands of years may be like a time bomb about to go off. The CO_2 comes mostly from decaying plants that died long ago. When permafrost thaws, this CO_2 is released into the atmosphere. This release speeds up warming in the region, causing even more thawing.

A block of melting permafrost collapsed on the Arctic coast of Alaska, in the far northwestern United States.

VII. THE FUTURE

Why are habitats important to humans?

The loss of habitats affects humans in ways almost beyond counting. When grasslands turn into desert, people and animals risk starvation.

Natural habitats not only provide clean air, water, food, building materials, and scenic beauty but also other reasons one might not expect. For example, some important medicines are made from chemicals that were found in rain forest plants. Who knows what undiscovered benefits are yet to be found in these habitats?

Forest habitats recycle much of the water that becomes rain. In some parts of the Amazon region in South America, half the water vapor in the **atmosphere** comes from the rain forest. Without forests to recycle water, terrible **droughts** would be more widespread in many regions.

Wetland habitats along coasts shield communities from **storm surges** and floods by soaking up water. Almost 70 percent of people in the U.S. state of Louisiana live within 50 miles (80 kilometers) of the northern coast of the Gulf of Mexico. Without these wetlands, millions of people are in greater danger from hurricanes and the damaging storm surges they bring.

A swamp in Louisiana, on the Gulf Coast, protects people from the worst flooding from storms and hurricanes.

How can we help?

All people can help combat climate change and global warming by changing little things in their everyday lives. If everybody did a little, it would add up to a big benefit for the world's natural habitats.

Generating electric power often involves burning such **fossil fuels** as coal and natural gas, producing **carbon dioxide** (CO_2) and contributing to global warming. By reducing our use of electric power, we can help reduce the production of **greenhouse gases.**

Turn off lights when they are not needed. Replace older lights with new, energy-saving light bulbs. Turn off computers and other electronic devices when no one is using them. Unplug phone chargers when electronic devices are not being powered up. Take shorter showers to save fuel used to heat water. Many of these tips will also help save money.

Nature centers and conservation groups do more direct work to help preserve valuable habitats. Try to find a local center where you can visit or even volunteer. The centers will help you discover many different ways you can help protect and improve the natural habitats around your home.

Helping out

Famed naturalist Jane Goodall founded Roots & Shoots, a program in which young people around the world help animals and their habitats. Roots & Shoots involves nearly 150,000 young people in more than 120 countries. Kids work with adult mentors to help preserve habitats in their own communities. For example, members have planted thousands of new trees across the United States. In Thailand, a project leader taught children about the "three R's"—reducing, reusing, and recycling—that help our environment.

GLOSSARY and RESOURCES

acidic High in acid, a damaging liquid capable, when strong enough, of eating away solids and burning skin.

algae (singular, **alga**) Simple life forms that live in oceans, lakes, rivers, ponds, and moist soil. Some algae are tiny and consist of just one cell, but others are large and contain many cells.

amphibian Cold-blooded animals having a moist skin without scales. Frogs, toads, newts, and salamanders are amphibians. Their eggs are laid in water, where the young hatch and usually develop as tadpoles that have gills for breathing.

atmosphere The mass of gases that surrounds a planet.

average temperature A temperature for a given time period. For example, in a month, the temperature for each day is totaled, and that number is divided by the number of days in the month, to get the average temperature.

boreal Northern forest mainly consisting of conifer (cone-bearing) trees.

carbon dioxide A colorless gas with no smell found in the atmosphere. On Earth, green plants must get carbon dioxide from the atmosphere to live and grow. Animals breathe out the gas when their bodies change food into energy. Carbon dioxide is also created by burning things that contain the element carbon.

climate The weather of a place averaged over a length of time.

coral reef A type of underwater structure largely made of a framework of limestone skeletons from ocean animals called corals.

drought A long period of dry weather.

ecosystem A system made up of a group of living beings and their *environment* (surroundings).

equator The great circle of Earth that lies halfway between the North and South poles.

extinct When every member of a *species* (kind) of living thing has died out.

food chain A series of stages energy goes through in the form of food. In one simple example, grass is eaten by a rabbit. The rabbit, in turn, is eaten by a fox. This series—grass, rabbit, fox—forms a food chain.

fossil fuel Coal, oil, or natural gas.

fungi (singular, **fungus**) A group of living things that produce spores and get nourishment from dead or living organic matter. Mushrooms, molds, mildews, and yeasts are fungi.

greenhouse gas Any gas that warms Earth's atmosphere by trapping heat.

hibernate To spend a season in a state of deep sleep.

humidity Moisture in the air.

invasive Living things that spread rapidly in new environments.

keystone species A type of animal that is unusually important to the habitat it lives in.

migration Moving from one place or region to another.

permafrost A layer of permanently frozen ground.

prairie A large area of level land with grass but few or no trees.

precipitation Moisture in the form of rain, snow, sleet, ice, or hail.

predator An animal that eats other animals.

species A group of animals or plants that have certain physical characteristics in common.

storm surge A rapid rise in sea level that happens when winds drive ocean waters ashore.

topsoil The rich upper part of the soil.

wetland A swamp, marsh, or bog.

Books:

Green, Dan, and Simon Basher. *Climate Change*. New York: Kingfisher, 2014.

Kurlansky, Mark, and Frank Stockton. *World without Fish*. New York: Workman Pub.,

McPherson, Stephanie Sammartino. *Arctic Thaw: Climate Change and the Global Race for Energy Resources*. Minneapolis: Twenty-First Century Books, 2015.

Rothschild, David de. *Earth Matters*. New York: DK Pub., 2011.

Tomecek, Steve. *Global Warming and Climate Change*. New York: Chelsea House, 2012.

Websites:

NASA – Climate Change and Global Warming
http://climate.nasa.gov/

National Park Service – Climate Change
http://www.nps.gov/subjects/climatechange/

United States Environmental Protection Agency – A Student's Guide to Global Climate Change
http://www.epa.gov/climatestudents/

United States Environmental Protection Agency – Climate Impacts on Ecosystems
http://www.epa.gov/climatechange/impacts-adaptation/ecosystems.html

Think about it:

Think about the things that you need to survive in your habitat. Make a list of them. For example, you cannot survive without fresh water and air, so be sure to list them.

How might each of the things you need in your habitat be affected by climate change? In fact, is climate change already affecting your habitat?

INDEX

A

acidic seawater, 4, 12, 14
algae, 18-19, 36
Alpine tundra, 38-39
Amazon rain forest, 26-27, 42
animals and plants. See habitats
Arctic region, 4, 36, 40-41
Atacama Desert, 7
atmosphere, 4, 12, 40, 43

B

bison, 34
bleaching of coral, 14
boreal forests, 28-29

C

Canada, 28-29
carbon dioxide (CO_2), 4, 44; deserts and, 6; grasslands and, 30; oceans and, 12, 14; tundra and, 40
climate change, 4, 47; ways to fight, 44-45. See also habitats
conservation, 44-45
coral reefs, 4-5, 14-15

D

desertification, 10, 30, 42
deserts, 4, 6-11, 30
drought, 18, 20, 26, 42
ducks, 20-21

E

ecosystems, 6, 16, 18
extinction, 8, 12, 16, 23

F

fires, 6, 24, 30
floods, 18, 20
fog, 9
food chains, 4, 16
food web, 16
forests, 24-30, 42
fossil fuels, 40, 44
freshwater habitats, 18-23

G

glaciers, 18
global warming. See climate change
Gobi, 10
Goodall, Jane, 45
grasslands, 4, 10, 26, 28, 30-35, 43
Great Barrier Reef, 5, 14-15
greenhouse gases, 44

H

habitats, 4; desert, 6-11; forest, 24-29; freshwater, 18-23; grassland, 31-35; importance of, 42-43; ocean, 4-5, 12-17; tundra, 36-41; ways to help, 44-45
hibernation, 36
Himalaya, 38-39

I

insects, 6, 22, 24
invasive plants, 6

J

jellyfish, 17

K

keystone species, 16

L

Louisiana, 42

M

migration, 20, 32

N

Namib, 8-9
nature centers, 44

O

oceans, 4-5, 12-15

P

permafrost, 36, 40-41
plankton, 16
Prairie Pothole region, 20-21
precipitation, 38
pufflegs, black-breasted, 27
pupfish, Devils Hole, 23

Q

quiver trees, 8

R

rain forests, 26-27, 42
Roots & Shoots program, 45

S

Sahara, 10-11
Serengeti, 32-33
snow, 38, 40
soil, 10, 18
storm surges, 42

T

tree line, 38
trees. See forests; quiver trees
tundra, 4, 28, 36-41

V

Valley of the Moon, 6-7

W

wetlands, 18, 42
wildebeest, 32-33

Z

zebra, 32-33

Maplewood Public Library
7550 Lohmeyer Ave.
Maplewood, MO 63143